What HMOs Don't Want You to Know About Your Pap Smear!

What HMOs Don't Want You to Know About Your Pap Smear!

And what every woman <u>should</u> know

By C. Arthur Ellis, Jr., M.A., M.S., C.T., Ph.D. and Leslie E. Ellis, M.R.C, L.M.H.C., Ph.D.

Writers Club Press
New York Lincoln Shanghai

What HMOs Don't Want You to Know About Your Pap Smear!
And what every woman <u>should</u> know

Writers Club Press
an imprint of iUniverse, Inc.

For information address:
iUniverse, Inc.
2021 Pine Lake Road, Suite 100
Lincoln, NE 68512
www.iuniverse.com

This book is strictly educational in nature and is produced to give the consumer a better understanding of her Pap smear. It is in no way intended to give medical advice. For medical advice, and to answer any specific questions regarding your Pap smear, you should see your physician.

ISBN: 0-595-28033-1

Printed in the United States of America

Contents

Preface

So what does your HMO not want you to know about your Pap smear? They pay for you to have one every year, right? And your doctor gives you the results, right?

True. But once you read this book and learn more about your Pap smear, you will begin making decisions about your health care that could very well increase costs for your insurance provider—that's what they don't want you to know. After all, their primary goal is to reduce their costs, not to give you the best medical care possible.

Contrary to what most insurance companies—particularly HMOs—would have you believe, the largest increases in health care costs in providing Pap smear tests over the past five years has resulted not from increases in physician or laboratory charges, but from the availability of new technologies that can greatly improve the traditional Pap test that was first developed in the 1950s.

Since I have spent ten years in the practice of cytology—the field of medical technology that screens slides for cancer—I have seen numerous instances of women receiving less than optimal medical care. Not because of poorly trained technologists or physicians, but because of a lack of consumer knowledge—not knowing what questions to ask to better direct their health care.

While no one but your physician is qualified to deliver your medical care, knowing the right questions to ask about your Pap smear can save your life.

Hopefully, reading this book will help you receive the health care you deserve.

C. Arthur Ellis, Jr.,
M.A., M.S., C.T., Ph.D.

Introduction

By reading this book, you have just taken the second step that may very well save your life. What was the first step? Having a Pap smear in the first place.

In the United States, the death rate from cervical cancer (the type of cancer most often found by using the Pap smear) has decreased at least 60% during the fifty years since Dr. George Papanicolaou first developed the test in the 1950s.

In the last few years, a new procedure with the trade name of Thin-Prep™ has allowed for far superior detection of adenocarcinoma, the kind of glandular cancer that was previously very difficult to detect with the traditional Pap smear.

But these dramatic results are possible only when you go to your physician each year and ask for a Pap smear. And your role in managing your own health care doesn't end there.

Being able to read your Pap smear report and understand what it means makes you an educated health care consumer, and gives you a tremendous advantage in taking charge of your own health care management.

By the time you have read this book:

- You will understand quite a bit more about your own Pap smear results than you have ever understood before.

- You will get answers to what your Pap smear diagnosis means.

- You will learn what you can do to make sure you have a correct diagnosis.

- You will understand what new technologies are available to diagnose your Pap smear.

Finally, and most important of all, you will learn how to talk with your doctor to ensure that you have the best medical care that you can get, regardless of limitations placed on your health care by managed health care plans.

Knowing how to work with your doctor by asking the right questions may very well save your life.

What is a pelvic examination?

The pelvic exam is a "check-up" of your vagina (inside and outside), cervix (opening of the uterus), and uterus (womb).

Your physician will look inside the vagina with a speculum, a plastic instrument that lets the practitioner see inside the vagina. He or she may also take tests at that time, including a Pap smear and special tests for Gonorrhea and Chlamydia if indicated.

During the examination of your vagina and labia, the physician will also look for syphilis or herpes sores, as well as genital warts that indicate the presence of HPV (Human Papillomavirus).

During the pelvic exam, drops of discharge from the vagina may be collected and examined under the microscope to check for Candida (yeast), Trichomonas, and bacterial vaginosis.

The second part of the pelvic examination is a manual examination inside the vagina to check the uterus, fallopian tubes and ovaries for normal development.

A thorough pelvic examination is an essential requirement of an annual OB-GYN exam.

What is a Pap smear?

The Pap smear is a test, first developed in the 1950s by Dr. George Papanicolaou, that checks for changes in the cells of your cervix—the lower part of the uterus that opens into the vagina—by taking a sample of these cells, preserving them, and examining them under the microscope.

This sample of cells preserved on a Pap smear gives the clinician a picture of the kinds of cells your body is producing, and is a good indicator of whether the underlying cells are normal or abnormal.

In addition to the traditional Pap smear, a newer technique, with the trade name of ThinPrep™, employs a vial of liquid preservative in which the collection brush is swished around to disperse the sample cells. The bottle is then sealed and sent to the laboratory for processing by a patented process resulting in a single layer of cells, rather than the piled up cells of a traditional Pap smear. This sample may also be used for reflex DNA testing for HPV, as well as to prepare a cell block (a kind of "micro-biopsy" made from the collected cells) if the Pap smear is abnormal. These additional tests give ThinPrep™ distinct advantages over a traditional Pap smear.

How is a Pap done?

Your health care provider can perform a Pap test during a pelvic exam. It is a quick test that takes only a few minutes.

You will be asked to lie down on an exam table and put your feet in holders called "stirrups," letting your knees fall to the side. A sheet will cover your legs and stomach.

The health care provider will put an instrument called a "speculum" into your vagina, opening it to see the cervix and to do the Pap test.

The practitioner will use a special stick, brush or swab to take a few cells from inside and around the cervix. The cells are placed on a small glass slide, or swished around in a special collection container, then checked by a lab to make sure they are healthy.

While painless for most women, a Pap test can cause mild to moderate discomfort and bleeding for some, especially those who have what is known as a "friable," or brittle, cervix.

Who is qualified to take my Pap smear?

Performing this procedure correctly requires a skilled medical practitioner for the following reasons:

- If the cells are not collected from the cervical area—the area where cancer cells most often occur—the Pap smear may be interpreted as normal, even if cancer cells are present in the patient.

- If the specimen sits too long on the slide without being sprayed by a fixative or preserving agent, the cells dry out and become "air dried," causing a distortion in their appearance and rendering them difficult or impossible to diagnose.

- If the Pap smear is spread too thick, it becomes much more difficult to screen for cancer cells, since the cancerous cells may be buried underneath normal cells.

The trained medical practitioner has a better chance of collecting cancer cells so that they may be diagnosed when they are sent out to the laboratory. Up to 2/3 of false negative Pap smears result from factors related to the collection procedure.

Because of the skill required, doctors who specialize in performing pelvic examinations and who are trained in "Obstetrics and Gynecology" are much more likely to prepare a better Pap smear.

Making certain that your doctor is Board Certified in his or her profession is critical to your health care, regardless of whether your HMO provides for this kind of practitioner or not.

Your Board Certified physician may employ a trained medical professional to take your Pap smear. At all times, however, the physician is responsible for your medical care and should be available to answer your questions.

Who diagnoses a Pap smear?

It is important to understand the difference between "screening" a Pap smear and "diagnosing" a Pap smear.

Technically, only a pathologist can diagnose a Pap smear. In practicality, however, most Pap smears are never seen by a physician, even though the diagnostic results appear over a physician's electronic signature.

This is because Pap smears are initially screened by cytotechnologists, highly trained medical technologists who look at the slides and refer what they believe to be abnormal cases to a pathologist.

While there are quality control procedures in place to re-screen at least 10% of all slides originally screened as negative or normal, the remaining 90% of cases screened as normal are signed out without being reviewed by a physician.

In all cases, however, your physician can ask for a second screening and/or review by a pathologist, regardless of the initial screening results.

The final results of an abnormal Pap smear will be reported out only after being reviewed by a pathologist.

Why do I need a Pap test?

A Pap test can save your life. It can be used to detect cancer of the cervix—a common cancer in women—before it invades other parts of your body. If caught early, treatment for cancer of the cervix can be easier, and the chances of curing the disease are far greater.

More recent advances in technology have improved the chances of picking up glandular lesions, such as Adenocarcinoma, that are difficult to detect on traditional Pap smears.

Pap tests can also be used to detect infections and inflammation, as well as abnormal cells that can progress to cancer.

Women who plan to become pregnant should consult their physician about the advisability of a Pap smear since certain diseases, such as Herpes, can affect the baby. In the case of pregnancy, more specific tests for these diseases are also available, and are an important part of prenatal care.

Do all women need Pap tests?

It is important for all women to have Pap tests, along with pelvic exams, as part of their routine health care. You need to have a Pap test if you are over 18 years old.

If you are under 18 years old, and are, or have been, sexually active, you also need a Pap test.

There is no age limit for the Pap test. Even women who have gone through menopause need to get Pap tests.

Women with hysterectomies are not immune to cancer, particularly if they had cancer prior to the hysterectomy, if their hysterectomy is partial—leaving a portion of the cervix intact—or if they are heavy smokers.

Women who are infected with <u>HIV</u>, the virus that causes AIDS, are more at risk for developing cancer of the cervix and other cervical diseases.

The U.S. Centers for Disease Control and Prevention recommends that HIV positive women have an initial Pap test, and then another one 6 months later. If both of these Pap tests show no cancer or other problems, then the frequency of the test can be reduced to once a year.

I've had a hysterectomy. Do I need a Pap?

While Pap smears on patients who have had a hysterectomy with no prior diagnosis of cancer are rare, women who have had a hysterectomy should talk with their health care provider about whether they need to continue having routine Pap tests—especially if there is a family history of squamous cell carcinoma or a history of heavy smoking.

If the hysterectomy was performed because a woman had cancer or a pre-cancerous condition, the upper end of the vagina closest to where the uterus was removed still needs to be tested for abnormal changes.

Women who have had a total hysterectomy, removing both their uterus and cervix, may not need routine Pap tests. The presence of endocervical cells in Pap smears on these women, however, indicates that the cervix was not totally removed, and can still be a source of abnormal cells.

Women who have had only the uterus removed, while still retaining their cervix, need regular Pap tests.

It is important for all women who have had a hysterectomy to have regular pelvic exams.

How often do I need to get a Pap test?

The College of American Pathologists recommends that you have a Pap smear and a pelvic examination each year. Since cervical cancer takes time to develop to a deadly stage, early detection—when the cancer is not at the invasive stage—gives you a better chance of being cured.

Many health care providers tell women to get a Pap test every year, even if their last Pap smear was normal.

Some health care providers may recommend a Pap test every 1 to 3 years after you have had 3 normal Pap tests for 3 years in a row. Consistency of repeated normal results is extremely important, since an abnormal Pap may have been missed in any given year.

Talk with your health care provider about what is best for you.

Above all, if you are a Medicare patient and are worried about coverage for your Pap smear, consult your physician, since there are exceptions to how often you can have a Pap smear if you have had a previous abnormal result.

What if my provider won't pay for my Pap smear?

Health plans vary widely in what they will pay for. As mentioned earlier, Medicare will not currently pay for an annual Pap smear for those covered under the plan unless there are special circumstances that, by Medicare guidelines, qualify for more frequent tests.

The important thing to keep in mind is that the cost of a traditional Pap smear is not great. Regardless of whether your insurance pays for the Pap or not, you should have it done every year, so try to budget for an annual exam.

Is there anything I need to do before having a Pap?

For two days before the Pap test, you should not douche or use vaginal creams, suppositories, foams or vaginal medications (for example, for a yeast infection).

It is also best to not use any vaginal deodorant sprays or powders for two days before your test since these agents contain microscopic particles that could interfere with the screening process. They can also cause irritation of the vaginal lining, which could result in erroneous reporting of your Pap smear results.

Do not have sexual intercourse within 24 hours of your Pap test. Sperm and lubricants can make the Pap smear difficult to diagnose.

You should not have a Pap test while you are having your period. The best time to have one is between 10 and 20 days after the first day of your last period. A Pap smear that is heavily obscured with blood may produce unreliable results since it is far more difficult to diagnose. This is true even with the new kinds of Pap smears using monolayer (single layer) techniques, since specimens taken during times of heavy bleeding may have cellular changes that do not appear normal.

Should I tell my doctor about any problems?

Yes! You must! If you have had any of the following, make sure your doctor knows:

- Previous abnormal Pap.

- Bleeding when you have sexual intercourse.

- Bleeding between menstrual periods.

- Warts on the outside of your vagina.

- Pain during sexual intercourse.

- Pain at any time in your lower back.

- Any treatment for cancer (chemical or radiological).

In addition to the above, be sure to tell your doctor about any changes in your health that you have observed, whether or not you believe the changes are relevant to your examination.

What happens after the Pap is done?

The results of your Pap report will determine the course of your treatment, if any:

- If the cells appear normal, no treatment is needed.

- If an infection is present, treatment is prescribed.

- If the cells look abnormal, or not healthy, more tests may be needed.

A Pap test is not 100% accurate all of the time, so it is always important to talk to your health care provider about the results of your report.

Since almost all Pap smears are initially screened by cytotechnologists (medical technologists specifically trained to screen Pap smears), you may want to ask that a cytopathologist (a trained physician specializing in cytopathology) look at your slide. This adds an extra level of protection for your diagnosis, and should be insisted upon if you have a normal result followed by an abnormal result, or if you have a history of cervical cancer in your family.

Alternately, you could ask that the slide be sent to another laboratory for a second opinion. Slides undergoing two screenings are much more likely to detect an abnormality—if it is present on the slide.

While these requests may generate additional charges, your health care is worth the expense.

What kinds of results are reported on a Pap smear?

A pap smear "diagnosis" does not mean the same thing as a diagnosis in other areas of medicine. The Pap smear is a way to "screen" for diseases. Following an abnormal report, it is necessary to follow up with other medical care to definitely establish what is properly called a "diagnosis."

In other words, this means that a Pap smear is used to wave a flag for the health car professional to proceed further with your medical care.

For many years, the language used to report Pap smear results was inconsistent and confusing. People in the medical field did not speak the same language.

In 1998, however, professionals in the field of Pap smears (pathologists and cytopathologists) gathered to set up a single system of reporting results on Pap smears to avoid confusion in terminology.

The system these medical professionals developed is called "The Bethesda System," named after the town, Bethesda, Maryland, where the conference was held.

The system established a standard way to report Pap smear results, allowing laboratories and physicians to use the same language.

Since its original creation, The Bethesda System has undergone numerous refinements, and is continuously updated as new information is gained from research in cytopathology.

The Bethesda System begins with a category for normal Pap smears and continues on to report those that have benign changes (usually from infections), to those that are abnormal (atypical), to those that are highly abnormal (dysplasia of several kinds), to cancer (carcinoma or adenocarcinoma).

How can I read my Pap smear report?

The best person to help you understand your Pap report is your physician. However, the following list of diagnoses given on Pap reports will assist you in understanding the terminology your physician will use.

Your Pap smear results will fall into one of the following diagnostic categories.

Summary of Descriptive Diagnoses

- Within Normal Limits (WNL)

- Benign or Reactive Cellular Changes (BCC OR RCC)

- ASCUS (Atypical Squamous Cells of Undetermined Significance):
    —favor reactive process (also called ASC-US)
    —favor dysplasia (also called ASC-H if HSIL cannot be excluded)

- AGUS (Atypical Glandular Cells of Undermined Significance):
    —favor reactive process
    —favor dysplasia

- LSIL (Low Grade Squamous Intraepithelial Lesion)
    —Mild dysplasia, with or without HPV changes

- HSIL (High Grade Squamous Intraepithelial Lesion)
    —Moderate dysplasia

- SCC (Squamous Cell Carcinoma)
  Adenocarcinoma
  > —endocervical
  > —endometrial

- Carcinoma in situ

- Invasive Carcinoma

Depending upon the laboratory issuing the report, there may be minor variations in the wording of these diagnoses, but most laboratories follow this format.

What do these diagnoses mean?

- If your report reads "Within Normal Limits (WNL)", then your Pap smear is normal and no evidence of cancer was found on the slide.

- If your report reads "Benign or Reactive Cellular Changes (BCC or RCC)," this means that you may have an infection or other problem that is causing the cells to change their normal appearance.

- If your report reads "ASCUS", this means that your Pap smear has some changes that are not strictly normal, but that it is uncertain what the changes are. There is a tendency in cytology to move away from diagnosing this category since it can be confusing and has been used as a "catchall" category when a more definite diagnosis could not be rendered. The physician will call you into the office for further evaluation, especially if the report adds, "favor dysplasia," or the diagnosis of ASC-H is given.

- If your report reads "AGUS," this means that your Pap smear has some abnormal glandular changes. Many health care practitioners will call you into the office for further diagnostic procedures within a very short time of receiving these results, especially if the report reads, "favor dysplasia," since glandular lesions are taken very seriously and could be an indicator of Adenocarcinoma.

- If your report reads "LSIL," this means that you have changes that need to be more closely followed than ASCUS. This diagnosis may continue to mention possible presence of HPV, a common cause of this abnormal change.

- If your report reads "HSIL," this means that your changes are considered pre-cancerous to the point that your doctor will want to perform a biopsy and look at the suspected area.

- If your report reads "Squamous Cell Carcinoma" or "Adenocarcinoma," your doctor will want to immediately schedule you for a biopsy and possible follow-up surgery.

- "Carcinoma in situ (CIS)," and "invasive carcinoma" are both extremely serious and demand immediate medical follow-up. There is some disagreement among practitioners about the validity of invasive carcinoma being diagnosed on a Pap smear, since most maintain that this diagnosis should be reserved for a biopsy.

What do these other things on my report mean?

In addition to the screening diagnosis, the Pap report gives additional information that you should be aware of:

- **Specimen Adequacy:** This gives a statement of how adequate the specimen was for evaluation by the practitioner. Sometimes the specimen is air-dried, obscured by blood or inflammation, or too scant to evaluate. Adequacy ranges from "Satisfactory," to "Satisfactory but Limited by (with reason for limitation)," to "Unsatisfactory for Evaluation (with reason for unsatisfactory determination)." A specimen may also be limited by "lack of endocervical cells", a remark that particularly disturbs many physicians since the endocervix is a common site of cancer and missing cells from this area could mean missing cancer cells.

- **Benign or reactive cellular changes:** These changes are often associated with organisms such as Chlamydia, Herpes, Trichomonas or Candida (yeast). A Pap smear is not the best way to detect these organisms, so they should be confirmed by other testing methods.

Changes can also be caused by such things as the presence of an IUD (intrauterine device), or mechanical or chemical injury (douches).

What do abnormal Pap results mean?

A health care provider may tell you that your Pap test result was "abnormal," which, as you have learned previously, does not necessarily mean that you have cancer.

Abnormal cells do not always turn into cancer. Also, some conditions are more likely than are others to turn into cancer.

If you have abnormal results, be sure to talk with your health care provider to find out what they mean and what you need to do (if anything) about it. Given any abnormal diagnosis, your physician should schedule follow-up to monitor the changes.

If you are still not satisfied, seek a second opinion.

What should I do if my Pap report is not normal?

If the Pap test shows a minor change in the cells of the cervix, the test may be done again.

If the test shows a major change in the cells of the cervix, the health care provider may perform a colposcopy. This is a procedure done in an office or clinic with an instrument called a colposcope that acts like a portable microscope, allowing the health care provider to look closely at the vagina and the cervix.

Your health care provider may also take a small amount of tissue from the cervix (called a biopsy) to examine for any abnormal cells that may be pre-cancerous.

What if my Pap smear is normal after being abnormal?

This can be a perfectly normal finding. On the other hand, it could be a false negative result, in which an abnormality is missed. This occurs in approximately 4% of all Pap smears.

Since taking a chance is not the best thing to do, you have choices in managing your own health care:

- Ask for a second opinion on the normal Pap smear.
- Follow up with still another Pap smear in 3 to 6 months following the normal Pap results.

If you cannot persuade your physician to get a second opinion or follow you closely, you probably need another physician—especially if you have a history of abnormal Pap smears.

What is a false positive or false negative?

A false positive Pap test happens when a woman is told she has abnormal cells, but the cells are in fact normal. A false positive result means that there is no problem, yet medical intervention may occur when it is not necessary.

A false negative Pap test happens when a woman is told her cells are normal, when in fact there is a change in the normal, healthy cells. This means there may be a problem needing immediate attention, and it is not given.

There are many things that can interfere with accurate Pap test results. This is why women need to be sure to get regular Pap tests. Having regular Pap tests increases a woman's chances that any problems will be picked up over the course of time. Having a second screening of the Pap smear also improves the reliability of the results.

Since Pap smear results are <u>screening</u> results, not <u>diagnostic</u> results, they should never be used as a basis for surgery without a confirmation of the diagnosis with a biopsy.

Can anything improve the accuracy of a Pap?

While the standard Pap test is very good at detecting abnormal changes, new methods are being developed to improve their accuracy. The Food and Drug Administration (FDA) has approved several new methods to help reduce false negative Pap test results.

One is called the Thin-Prep™ Pap test, where cervical cells are preserved in a solution, then sent to the laboratory where they are placed on the glass slide by a special machine that spreads the cells in a monolayer (single layer). This may make it easier to detect abnormal cells, especially in the case of glandular lesions such as Adenocarcinoma, which are better preserved by this method.

Other methods use computers to scan the cervical cells to look for abnormal cells. Two computer "re-screening" methods have been approved by the FDA—*PAPNET*™ and the *AutoPap*™ *300 QC*. Research is being done to find out if they are in fact more accurate than the standard Pap test.

Failing using these newer procedures, asking for a cytopathologist to take a second look at your slide, or having a second opinion at another laboratory, will increase your chances of having an accurate diagnosis on your Pap smear.

Is it possible my lab report is wrong?

There have been cases of erroneous findings resulting in the death of the patient. Largely because of these reports, the U.S. government and the College of American Pathologists (CAP) have taken steps to set up rigorous standards for clinical laboratories to follow.

While laboratories are not required to follow CAP standards, you are best advised to make certain your Pap is screened in a CAP-approved laboratory, whether or not your HMO pays for it.

Regardless of these safeguards, the Pap smear is not a perfect test, and the processing and reporting system is less than perfect as well.

Since the Pap smear follows a number of steps between being received in the laboratory and being reported out to the physician, errors can—and do—occur at any stage:

- When the slide is received in the laboratory, it may have been mislabeled in the physician's office. In this case, the lab would have no idea that they were reading the wrong slide.

- During processing, the wrong label could be put on the slide, confusing Pap smears between patients. This stage is referred to as "accessioning."

- During screening, the cytotechnologist could switch slides on the tray and confuse results between patients. This is most likely to occur in trays with two-slide cases for a single patient.

• During reporting out of results, the wrong results could be entered into the computer, especially if the results are manually entered.

For these reasons, it is prudent to ask for a pathologist review on a questionable result rather than to have another Pap smear immediately. Most physicians do this automatically if they have a report of a high grade lesion, but it does not hurt to confirm that this has been done.

In all cases, a Pap smear should be validated if it is reported out with any diagnosis that would require an invasive procedure, such as a biopsy.

What about the costs of these newer procedures?

All of these tests are more expensive than the traditional Pap smear, but some, especially ThinPrep™, are covered by most individual health insurance carriers.

Costs usually range between $75 to $125.

Check with your insurance provider to see if you have coverage for any of these tests.

Regardless of the cost, if you are at a high risk for cancer, isn't it worth paying the price to save your life?

Do sexually transmitted diseases cause cancer?

Certain genetic types of HPV (or the *humanpapilloma virus*) has been linked to cancer of the cervix.

HPV can cause wart-like growths on the genitals. When it is not treated or happens frequently, HPV can increase a woman's chances of developing cancer of the cervix.

HPV is very common, especially in younger women and women with more than one sexual partner. The use of condoms is not 100% effective against transmission of this disease, and it currently has no cure. Also, HPV may not be visible in a male, since it may be just inside his penis and be transmitted by his sperm.

It is important to understand that not all forms of HPV inevitably lead to cancer, and that even the ones with a high probability of becoming cancerous have been known to spontaneously revert to normal.

The best approach to handling a diagnosis of HPV is to ask your doctor for a DNA analysis. A type of DNA testing can be done on a ThinPrep™ sample without taking another specimen, giving this collection technique a distinct advantage in patients having a high risk for HPV.

What are the risk factors for cancer of the cervix?

Any woman can get cancer of the cervix. However, the chances of getting cancer of the cervix increase when a woman:

- Starts having sex before age 18.

- Has many sexual partners.

- Has sexual partners who have other sexual partners.

- Has had Humanpapilloma virus (HPV) or genital warts.

- Has had a sexually transmitted disease (STD).

- Is over the age of 60.

- Smokes.

APPENDIX

For more information...

1. National Women's Health Information Center (NWHIC) at 1-800-994-9662.

2. Cancer Information Service, NCI, NIH, HHS
    Phone Number: (800) 422-6237
    Internet Address: http://cis.nci.nih.gov/

3. American College of Obstetricians and Gynecologists (ACOG) Resource Center
    Phone Number: (800) 762-2264 ext. 192 (for publications requests only)
    Internet Address: http://www.acog.org/

4. National Cervical Cancer Coalition (NCCC)
    Phone Number: (800) 685-5531
    Internet Address: http://www.nccc-online.org/

5. American Society for Clinical Pathology (ASCP)
    Internet Address:
    http://www.ascp.org/general/

6. Internet Address: http://familydoctor.org/
    Search for Pap smear.

7. Internet Address: http://www.4woman.gov/faq/pap.htm

8. Information on ThinPrep™.
    Internet:
    http://www.questdiagnostics.
    com/hcp/topics/thinprep/thinprep.html

NOTES ON QUESTIONS TO ASK MY DOCTOR:

_____

_____

_____

_____

_____

_____

_____

_____

_____

_____

NOTES ON QUESTIONS TO ASK MY DOCTOR:

_____

_____

_____

_____

_____

_____

_____

_____

_____

NOTES ON QUESTIONS TO ASK MY DOCTOR:

_____

_____

_____

_____

_____

_____

_____

_____

_____

_____

0-595-28033-1

www.ingramcontent.com/pod-product-compliance
Lightning Source LLC
Chambersburg PA
CBHW021047180526

45163CB00005B/2315

9780595280339